Dog

Coloring Book For Adults

THIS BOOK BELONGS TO :

....

Lenard Vinci Press

Color Test Page

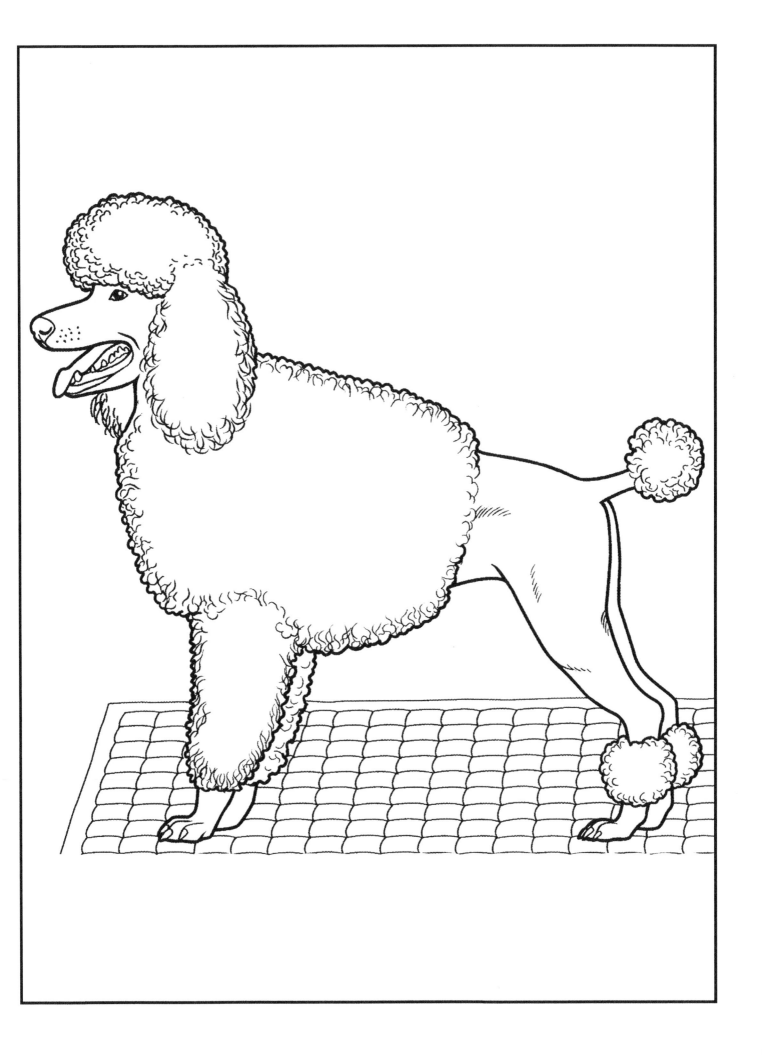

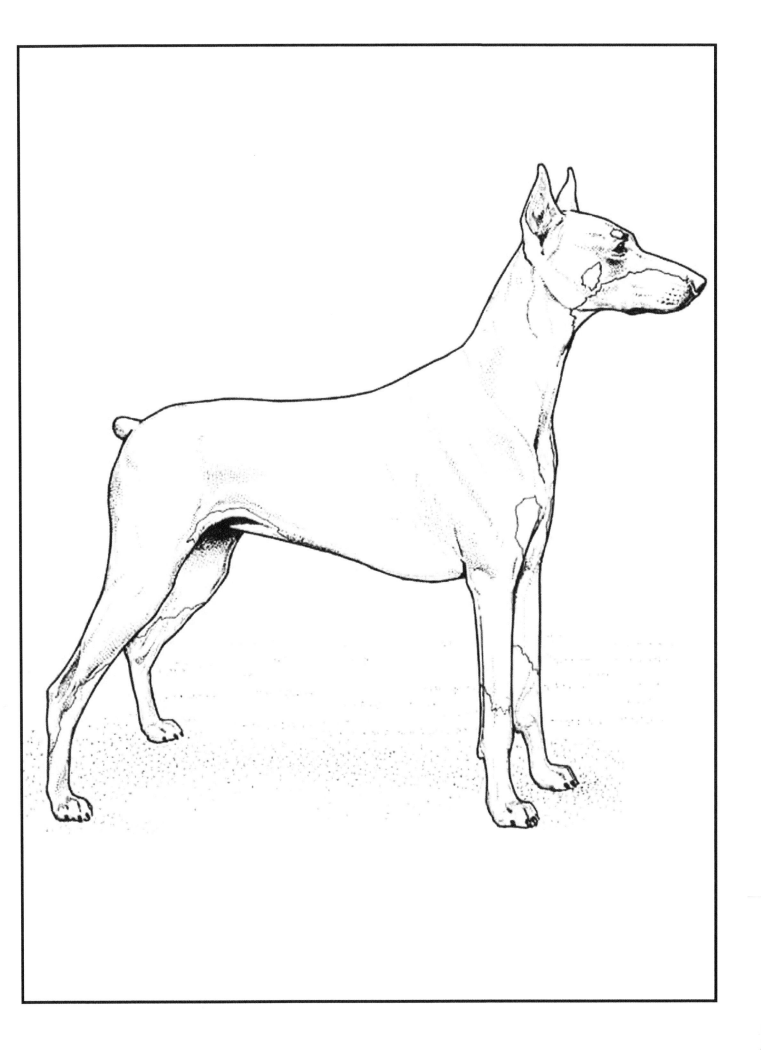

Thank You

We hope you enjoyed our book As a small family company, your
feedback is very important to us

Please let us know how you like
our book at:

lenardvincipress@gmail.com